I0491140

RİGHT MONEY

Table of Contents

Prologue 3

1. PART 5

GAINING INCOME FROM THE INTERNET: 5

ADVANTAGES AND DISADVANTAGES 5

    1. Developing an Application 8

    2. Blogging 9

    3. Selling Photos 10

    4. Marketing with Online Shops 10

    5. Selling Via Instagram 11

    6. Being a Sales Representative 11

    7. Writing an E Book 12

    8. Opening a YouTube Channel 12

    9. Futures and Options Market 13

    10. Drop-shipping 14

    11. Sales Partnership (Affiliate Marketing) 16

2. HOW CAN YOU PROVIDE 18

CAPITAL FOR YOUR NEW 18

BUSINESS? 18

    Ways to Provide Capital 19

    What is capital? 19

    Bank Credits 20

    Credit Cards 22

    Partnership 22

Modern Sources of Funds 23

Pension Accounts 23

3. PART 24

EXAMPLES OF BUSINESS 24

OPPORTUNITIES 24

1. Opening a Café 26

Helpful Advices 26

Cost 28

2. Opening a Photo Studio 29

Helpful Advices 29

Cost 31

3. Opening an Auto Wash Center 31

Helpful Advices 32

Cost 33

4. Being a Hawker's Trader 34

Helpful Advices 34

Cost 35

5. Opening a Stand 36

Helpful Advices 36

Cost 38

Epilogue 39

Prologue

There are many people who want to get rid of the world order we live in and the boundaries dictated by it and live an alternative life. Everyone's dream is different, but they all come together on the basis of getting rid of offices that restrict freedom of movement and money that makes our life harder. I wanted to show you ways to make money and your dreams come true.

Before beginning; I want to clarify something to avoid disappointment:

It is not a convenient way for those who want to be rich by not working hard. On the contrary, you will probably work a lot more than your salaried business life because it is your own business. It does not mean that being on the Internet does not have seriousness. A business calendar that you have to follow closely, a customer satisfaction that needs to be taken seriously, things like job follow up also apply to online jobs. The only difference is that it gives you space and time freedom, which is a terrific achievement in our business and a factor that lifts many obstacles in front of your dreams.

I will also tell you where to find the appropriate capital for the business you want to set up in this article. It is very important that you get this capital because you need a certain amount of savings even when you make money from the internet. You can also set up lower-budget jobs with the capital you will get. I will tell you how to work with the internet and how to get new opportunities by using technology at low cost.

1. PART

GAINING INCOME FROM THE INTERNET:

ADVANTAGES AND DISADVANTAGES

New Ways to Gain Income: Internet World The development of technology at a rapid pace continues to change our lives, our understanding of entertainment and work. Thanks to internet presence, this change has gained a great pace.

So now we have the opportunity to reach almost every human being in the world. With social media and search engines, we are confronted with a great deal of knowledge at an amazing rate. Of course, because the internet is so big, it has become possible to make profits from this field.

How do you earn money from the internet? Since the days when the Internet has entered our lives, marketing, content marketing and advertising. But before I go through these methods, I will elaborate a bit more. In this article, I will talk about the passive income-generating methods through the internet as well as the actual

execution of this business in real time. However, it is worth pointing out again that making money from the internet is not as easy as you might think. You must make a serious effort to earn money from the Internet and you must be on your own.

You may not have much knowledge to start this business, but you have an unmistakable enthusiasm and you must be absolutely sure. This will make it easier for you to take lessons from your mistakes throughout the process and learn the

truths.

Whether it is from the internet or from outside the internet today; If you want to be successful, you have to create a value that people can benefit from. At the beginning you should show maximum effort for minimum income, for example.

Hele is much more specific for this internet world. Because a certain amount of time is required to gain a certain mass and asset on the internet. This time is also directly proportional to your efforts.

Successful people succeed because they can put in a valuable service and product.

These people think every detail thinly and they do not pursue money immediately.

At the end of success, you know that you have brought in the material gain.

There are different ways to earn money from the Internet, and it is possible to say

that these roads are increasing day by day. There are some ways in which you can

really make money and are accepted all over the world. Particularly in the last period of social media influences, the fastest and easiest ways to earn money from the

internet is usually done through social media platforms. Apart from the use of social

media platforms, there are ways to make money from the internet such as blogging,

photo sales, application development, sales partnership, drop-shipping, futures and

options market or freelance work from home in different jobs.

It should be noted that each of these methods has its own advantages and

disadvantages. Let's take a look at the ways in which you can profit from this internet,

one by one, in detail:

1. Developing an Application

If you have coding knowledge or if you have enough money to prepare the coding for another company, preparing the application and presenting it to the market is definitely in the top 3 among the recent ways to earn money from the Internet.

Google Play and App Store app stores for Android and IOS platforms are trading millions of dollars a day. It's still not too late to get involved in this market! If you have a good idea or believe that you can make a more advanced version of an existing game or application, you should absolutely log in to this sector.

The increase in the application sector is increasing every minute with the use of mobile phones.

We definitely recommend you do market research in the first place to prepare the right application and prevent the waste of your capital.

2. Blogging

You do not need serious coding or software knowledge to open a blog. You can even open a blog for free and create a simple blog. But if you want to make money from the internet by opening a blog, we recommend you take your own domain name and set your way for it.

If you are planning to open a blog, it is of course hard to be able to create a true mass of followers; However, if you have fun, fun or educational information that you can transfer to people, you will definitely attract visitors. It is also useful to say that blogs with experience usually grow in a shorter time.

Once you have succeeded in attracting visitors to your blog site, you can then advertise with your blog service through the advertising services.

3. Selling Photos

Do you have successful photos? Or do you get interesting professional photos? One of the most serious ways of earning money over the Internet is selling photos and pictures. There has been a significant increase in recent stock photo photos. There are even photographers who make thousands of dollars a month through platforms like Shutterstock and iStockPhoto.

Do not forget that you will face very serious competition to sell your photos. It is useful to say that even a photograph with the smallest flaw is hard to find.

4. Marketing with Online Shops

If you want to enter into e-commerce business but have problems about product and infrastructure, you can open a virtual market from Shopify, which serves through internet.

It is a much easier and more convenient way to make a store than you think. From these products you sell in the shopping system you open on these platforms, you earn commissions with changing per product. However, it will be difficult to make sales in the first place, you have to have entrepreneurial features.

If you have a moderate capital, it will certainly make more sense to open your own e-commerce site.

5. Selling Via Instagram

You are probably well aware of the recent rise of Instagram. This rise has allowed people to spend time in Instagram for a very long time. There are many entrepreneurs and businesses that have managed to achieve a serious income by opening a boutique in Instagram. Joining them is not as difficult as you might think.

Even with an average capital or even zero capital, you can start selling from Instagram. For further information on the subject, we recommend that you take a look at our Instagram Boutique guide.

6. Being a Sales Representative

Nearly every e-commerce platform that sells on the Internet has sales representatives that provide support through a form that meets the visitor. On some platforms the number of representatives is often even over 50. Most sales representatives work from home or office (remotely). Within this scope, you can find the e-commerce platforms by e-mail.

7. Writing an E Book

If you have the ability to write, you might consider writing an e-book. The e-book market is a huge area. For example, you can write a book on a technical subject to compete here. In this way you can make money even when you are asleep, you may need to spend a lot of effort writing the book. Once you have written the book and once it is published, you begin to make profits without doing anything. However, in order to purchase the book in the long term, your content should be good and useful. You can sell your e-book with Amazon Kindle or Apple iTunes Connect programs. It's also quite easy to sell e-books around here.

Membership fee is very small. In order to earn money from e-books, you have to have a high cultural capital than a financial one in order to write a good book. However, there is a topic that everyone knows very well. You can start writing a technical work related to your area of expertise.

8. Opening a YouTube Channel

YouTube channel is one of the ways to make the most fashion online money in recent years to turn. But we must emphasize that this is a long-term business. If you have dreamed of winning thousands of pounds in a night, it would be useful to lead another alternate. However, depending on the concept of your channel and the stability of your video upload, you can earn countable money from this business. So when YouTube is the subject, you have to find a certain concept and produce content by sticking to this concept. You can use anything you want. The important thing is that your videos have good quality and useful content. Thanks to the quality content, your growth rate will rise after a certain period of time.

9. Futures and Options Market

Option and futures are two similar sounding trading products, but are very different in practice. Buying an option gives a person the right, but not the obligation, to buy or sell something at a certain price in the future. A futures contract is an agreement by a buyer and seller that obliges them to buy or sell the underlying, at the price they agreed on, at a future date. Both products are used by retail traders and institutional investors, but often in different ways.

In order to make money, you have to choose the underlying asset correctly before trading in the binary option market. You need to trade with an underlying asset that you are familiar with or that you can make accurate estimates of the future of prices. You should then make a good market watch for this underlying asset, analyze the price graphs, and accurately estimate how the price will advance at the end of the payback period and buy the necessary option.

It is stated that the most important rule in binary option market is a good market watch. You should know the factors that affect the price of the base asset you choose, and you should follow developments about these factors. It seems that when the binary option is left on the edge and the transactions performed in the financial markets in general are considered, the market watch has a great proposition for all of them. It is known that the basic analysis gives much better results than the techniques, but still the most accurate result is obtained when two types of analysis are used together.

10. Drop-shipping

Dropshipping is a retail fulfillment method where a store doesn't keep the products it sells in stock. Instead, when a store sells a product, it purchases the item from a third party and has it shipped directly to the customer. As a result, the merchant never sees or handles the product.

The biggest difference between dropshipping and the standard retail model is that the selling merchant doesn't stock or own inventory. Instead, the merchant purchases inventory as needed from a third party usually a wholesaler or manufacturer to fulfill orders.

Less Capital Is Required – Probably the biggest advantage to dropshipping is that it's possible to launch an ecommerce store without having to invest thousands of dollars in inventory up front. Traditionally, retailers have had to tie up huge amounts of capital purchasing inventory. With the dropshipping model, you don't have to purchase a product unless you already made the sale and have been paid by the customer. Without major up-front inventory investments, it's possible to start a successful dropshipping business with very little money.

Easy to Get Started – Running an ecommerce business is much easier when you don't have to deal with physical products. Easy to Scale With a traditional business, if you receive three times as much business you'll usually need to do three times as much work. By leveraging dropshipping suppliers, most of the work to process additional orders will be borne by the suppliers, allowing you to expand with fewer growing pains and less incremental work. Sales growth will always bring additional work especially related to customer service but business that utilize dropshipping scale particularly well relative to traditional ecommerce businesses.

All these benefits make dropshipping a very attractive model to both beginning and established merchants. Unfortunately, dropshipping isn't all roses and rainbows. All this convenience and flexibility comes at a price.

11. Sales Partnership (Affiliate Marketing)

Affiliate marketing is the process of earning a commission by promoting other people's (or company's) products. You find a product you like, promote it to others and earn a piece of the profit for each sale that you make. The idea behind it is that you promote other people's products, often through an affiliate network, earning a commission if people actually end up buying thanks to your marketing.

It's based on revenue sharing. If you have a product and want to sell more, you can offer promoters a financial incentive through an affiliate program. If you have no product and want to make money, then you can promote a product that you feel has

value and earn an income from it as an affiliate marketer.

There are basically two sides of the affiliate marketing equation that you can choose from, assuming that you're not going to build an affiliate network such as

Commission Junction. You can become a merchant and have others promote your product, in exchange for giving them a commission from the sales that they make. Or, you can become an affiliate marketer for one or several products that you'd like to promote and market those to consumers, in order to make money.

While most people start by taking the affiliate route and it definitely is the easier path to take, building enough traffic to make a meaningful income just from affiliate sales isn't quick or easy.

2. HOW CAN YOU PROVIDE CAPITAL FOR YOUR NEW BUSINESS?

Ways to Provide Capital
What is capital?

It is one of the production factors necessary for the production to be done. It is possible to divide the capital into two as fixed and revolving capital. Fixed capital does not run out during its first use in production. Factories, machinery, equipment and other fixed assets are examples of this capital. The types of capital such as money, stocks, and receivables that are lost in the first use are called revolving funds.

Capital in terms of business; it is divided into self and foreign capital according to its sources. Equity is the value that the operator allocates to use for business, separating it from the wealth that it owns personally. In addition to equity capital, foreign borrowing by the operator and loans are called foreign capital.

If you want to start a business but you do not have enough money to pay for your work from your budget, then you will have to apply for foreign capital resources. The question of how to obtain these capital resources is curiosity.

I will also give you information on how to create this capital in this section. Starting a Business with Bank Credits

Although the conditions for getting a loan are challenging, there are many options for those who want to start a business when it comes to finding cash.

Capital is at the forefront of the issues that most people want to start a new business. Capital is a stepping stone when a job is successful. You will have to pay for the success, and the risk is inversely proportional to the capital you have. For that reason,

it is much easier for you to achieve success in large capital projects. For small businesses it is not raining from the heap, and to get a business credit it is necessary to overflow a certain amount of water. The banks' credit policies are very tight and this situation is challenging for entrepreneurs who want to get credit. Those who want to start a business need to be creative while looking for resources for their capital. At this point you can get help from the following options for getting credit or capital:

Bank Credits
Your local bank can offer you low interest rates and long-term repayment plans. It sounds good, but some entrepreneurs think that strict commitment regulations make it almost impossible to accept a loan.

The credit conditions of each bank are different, so go to the bank for optimal conditions. Start with your own personal bank. If the banker knows you, he or she can help you with your application more. State Credits Obtaining government-guaranteed loans similar to traditional bank loans is also a difficult and lengthy process. It is rare that no collateral is required before the credit is approved.

If you get a government loan you can get credit at low interest rates and long term repayment terms. You can get detailed information about the loans by reviewing the internet pages about small businesses. Borrowing from Family or Friends

The people you love most or your close friends want your business to be successful. For this reason, these people may be your closest and favorite source of funds. In exchange for your credits and gratitude these people will receive interest-free loans according to the funds of banks or money markets for loans.

Make sure you do it right. Prepare a written contract with a special reimbursement terms or a written order. On this count, you do not go against anybody.

If you mix work and personal, you can ruin your relationships. Housing Mortgage Having your home as a source is one of the fastest and easiest ways to make cash.

However, it should be remembered that in the past years many landlords have been in a difficult situation. For this reason, the banks have reduced the credit limit on real estate and have begun to impose the mortgage loan amount on the value of real estate value.

If your home is worth the collateral, think carefully before you risk your home. If things go wrong with your business, you may be at risk of losing your home, and at the same time you will be personally responsible for all payments.

Credit Cards

Personal and business credit cards may appear as an easy solution to meet your needs, but they can be very costly due to the high interest rates. Use credit cards sparingly and do not use it for long-term financing.

Partnership

If you want to share your future success with someone, you can consider cooperating with a partner who can put money into the business.

Be careful to find yourself a partner.

While your partner can provide cash, it can also bring new ideas about how the business will be managed. You have to share some of your issues with your partner, and you need to set some specific legal agreements that outline the role of your partner in the company.

Modern Sources of Funds

Web sites suddenly emerge and offer credit facilities to consumers. Some websites combine potential borrowers and issuers to provide unsecured credit over a three year fixed interest rate. Buyers report the maximum interest rate they are willing to pay and how much they can pay, and they bid for the loan when they will open the loan.

Pension Accounts

This should be the last resource to be applied. You have to put money on the side for your future. Even if you see your enterprise as your future, it can be wrong to think like that.

Some credit plans offer loans that match the values you specify. Principal and interest payments are made through salary cuts. Some credit schemes also require the immediate payment of the entire loan if you lose your job. So, I do not think you should lose your pension account to start a new business.

3. PART

EXAMPLES OF BUSINESS

OPPORTUNITIES

Low Cost High Income Business Examples There are always great business ideas for those who need serious capitalism. It is, of course, more difficult to find business ideas to be made with small capital. However, I always conduct research on the market and includes many business ideas to be made especially for small capital entrepreneurs.

A maximum of $ 20,000 dollars will be required for the works in this guide. However, some business ideas can be made even with 1-2 thousand dollars and you can easily make money with the right planning. When you look at business ideas you should not look only capital-focused. Your talents, education, and when you can separate it are very important to choose between these business ideas.

If you want to start a business with less capital, you can choose the one that suits you among these jobs by looking at the business ideas that are in this guide. Again, if you need to make a warning, do not just look at the work done with low capital, your talents and your skills are important. So do not try to do a job that does not fit you at all, just not your capital.

The most important feature of jobs that require less capital is that they have a low real estate and do not want to advertise or advertise in very high quantities. In some business sectors, your capital does not really matter. For this reason, you should always remember that if you want to achieve success in your business ideas, you should always take some care.

1. Opening a Café

Have you ever felt a desperate need for a change in your career? Have you ever wanted to quit your job instantly, and start doing something that fulfills you? You may be sitting at your desk right now thinking about starting your own business. Mind flooded with memories of times spent hanging out in cafes, it brings you to a realization: "I would like to open my own cafe!"

Helpful Advices

The very first thing you should take into account! Even if the place you have chosen to be your future cafe is in a perfect condition, you cannot just open it for business immediately. In case you decide to do that anyway, there is more than a 90% chance that you will fail before reaching six months of operation. Why? There is a reason the person selling their business to you is leaving that space. The neighborhood might be going through radical changes, customers may dislike some parts of their service; bad management and other issues could impose challenges for new business being started there. Even if the previous owner claimsopposite. You will need to find this bug, deal with it, differentiate from the previous owner, or at least make changes that will be registered.

It is realistic to open a cafe within three months (a very optimistic option) to eight months (a pessimistic option) from the moment you rented the space. For this period of time it is reasonable to have a discount for rent negotiated, or simply have enough money to start with.

Here are few examples of things you might need and their estimated delivery times: a new espresso machine (3 – 5 weeks), a customized bar and furniture (8 weeks), branded cups (4 weeks), a by-law approval of the construction from the Department of Hygiene (4 weeks), outdoor seating authorization (up to 12 weeks). Further regulations will depend on your location and country legislations.

To make customers search for you, you need to create a unique concept. Have a business plan ready, go the extra mile to make your customers experience something new and unexpected. They will come back for it.

First of all, define your target customer and create a concept that meets his needs. When are ready, create one strong sentence saying why is your café unique. This will help you concentrate in the future. Invest in yourself and your staff. Pay for good espresso and filter coffee brewing courses. You can try to convince an experienced barista to help you out in the beginning. If you want to learn to make nice latte art, you will need to buy 40 liters of milk, and practice. Just be ready for demanding customers and have high demands on yourself as well! Healthy self-criticism is good for you.

Cost

Opening a cafe is a long term investment. If you see it that way, you will agree it is worth it getting a new, quality machine that will last and will allow you to serve the coffee you want, without compromises. Why? Because coffee is the heart of a cafe business!

New coffee machines might be more expensive, but you pay the price for endurance of the machine's service. In case the machine brakes, you get a profit service on it. A new basic 2 group espresso machine can cost 2300 – 4 000 EUR without VAT. You can find better coffee machines for about 3 000 – 5 500 EUR, the great ones are priced at about 4 500 – 9 000 EUR and the fantastic ones up to 11 000 EUR without VAT.

It does not end with buying a coffee machine, though. You need one grinder – if you want to serve only one coffee. In case of two options for espresso you will need two grinders. Count in one more for filter options. Grinder prices range between 500 – 3000 EUR, depending on what do you expect from them, and what amount of coffee do you want to grind with them. If you want to offer decaffeinated coffee, you will need another grinder.

Next thing you want is a water filter. You can purchase one at 100 – 300 EUR, based on the water quality at your water source. It needs to be changed every 6 – 12 months. Well and then you need to equip your café with such things as a cooling showcase, fridges, ice machine, dishwasher, freezer and so on.

2. Opening a Photo Studio
Photography is a good career opportunity and maybe you want to pursue it. To become a successful photographer, you will need a successful photography studio!

Helpful Advices
Starting your own photography business is a great way to add a second income or a main income, if you work hard. While the photography market is competitive, many photography business owners have been able to find their niche and build a

sustainable career. Like most creative endeavors, you need to balance your passion for photography with real business skills in order to be successful.

To build and grow your business, you need both raw talent and a knack for marketing. One photographer we spoke with said an ability "to market yourself" was one of the most important factors in success. You should continually be working to improve your craft and evolving your product, and work consistently on your own branding, online marketing and people skills. Without the two, the results will likely just be an expensive hobby rather than a viable full-time business. So take these advices serious.

The gear you need for a new studio is only the gear that you will use in the studio. Ideally, a lot of what you have already you'll be able to repurpose. Don't invest in gear that only looks great and that you think you need because other studios have it. In the studio, you sometimes need two lights and sometimes five.

Working in the studio is different than working on location. In the studio, you can have gear that's a little less portable but much more sturdy and easy to use on a flat surface.

Another key element to making your studio location fun, easy and free of tech problems is the perfect tethering station you built. You may not be able to afford the fancy lights immediately or the expensive heavy-duty stands, but that doesn't mean, you can't start working in your studio immediately with the gear you already have.

Your studio shouldn't have only a space to do photography. It should also become your office and a convenient area for clients to hang out while they're waiting for you.

Be careful about these advices and be successful!

Cost

Quality photography equipment is notoriously expensive, so you'll want to start off with the minimum: Buying a $5,000 lens doesn't make sense if your business isn't making money yet. Many professional photographers say to plan on budgeting about

$10,000 to start your photography business.

3. Opening an Auto Wash Center

Opening a car wash business can be a fun, interesting, and profitable business for somebody with business smarts and perseverance. With the right location, good marketing, and top-notch service, you can draw in numerous customers who need their cars washed quickly, efficiently, and at a good price. However, opening a car wash business also requires a significant investment, good planning, and attention to detail in order to make your business profitable.

Helpful Advices

Even if you've worked at a car wash business, you'll need to be up to date on all the latest trends and technologies to have a good understanding of the industry. Visit other car washes and figure out the type of car wash you would like to open (e.g. self service, automatic, waterless, full detailing, etc.)

• For example, people use car washes more when the economy is doing well and

when motor vehicle sales are up. When people have more money to spend, they are more willing to pay for a car wash. Knowing the car sales statistics in

your area could help you predict success for your business.

• Talk to car wash owners, car wash suppliers, and car wash equipmentmanufacturers. You want to understand the car wash business from all sides

so you know what you are getting into.

• The International Carwash Association is a good resource to learn about theindustry and the current trends.

• Read Internet trend reports and business periodicals. Find out what the demographics are in your area and read up on how car wash businesses are doing in areas with similar demographics.

• Read business publications to find out what the newest materials and equipment are. The car wash industry is developing more energy efficient andenvironmentally friendly materials, so it's important to stay abreast of new developments.

In order for your business to be competitive, you need to thoroughly research the other car washes in your area. If you have already chosen a location for your car wash, scope out all the competition within a 5 mile Radius A business plan will help you get financing to start your car wash and think through the details of your business. Make your plan as detailed as possible. The business plan should include an introduction (3-5 pages), market analysis (9-22 pages), company description (1-2 pages), organization and management (3-5 pages), marketing and sales strategies (4-6 pages), product/service (4-10 pages), equity investment and funding request (2-4 pages), financial information (12-25 pages).

Cost

You can finance your new car wash through bank financing, a Small Business Association (SBA) loan, or through private investors. You will also need to have some cash of your own saved up to secure financing from others. The best way to do this is by presenting your business plan to your potential investor and show how your idea can be a viable business.

• A bank loan requires a loan-to-value ratio of 75%. You will need to come up with 25% of the fair market value and the bank will fund the other 75%. It will be harder for you to secure bank financing if you have never owned a business before.

4. Being a Hawker's Trader

A Market Hawker is an individual who is licensed to sell by retail from any allocated site within the precincts of an open-air market.

Helpful Advices

To obtain a license to act as a Market Hawker, an individual should make an application on the appropriate form to the Trade Licensing Unit. Attached to the application should be two passport photos of the applicant.

A Market Hawker using a motor vehicle to carry on his commercial activity shall have premises available where to garage the motor vehicle and store his goods. The address of the premises used for this purpose must be clearly indicated on the application. Any change in the vehicle or garage has to be notified to the Trade Licensing Unit within ten

(10) working days after the change occurs. An application cannot be accepted and processed by the Trade Licensing Unit if the address of the garage or any other address for the store where goods are to be stored are not given. The Trade Licensing Unit has the right to inspect such premises and to demand any documentation that proves the ownership of the premises when the application indicates the use of such premises by more than one licensee.

The license issued by the Trade Licensing Unit will indicate the Market Hawker as a non-food license Hawker or as a food related items license Hawker. In the case that this activity concerns the selling of food items prior approval by the Health Authorities must be obtained.

The use and provision of public utilities is prohibited. A license issued for a Market Hawker is a personal license which is not transferable and does not permit anybody else to act instead of the licensee.

Cost
€40 every three (3) years and to act as a market hawker from a fixed site in the open air market. But the costs and license fees can change.

5. Opening a Stand

Options for starting a cart or kiosk business include opening a permanent location in a mall and leasing a cart; buying a cart to use for outdoor events or on street corners; or renting a cart short-term.

"The least expensive option is to rent [a cart] for a short time and see how it goes,"

says Bruce Stockberger, owner of Stockberger Marketing Associates, a North Palm Beach, Florida, small-business marketing firm specializing in cart, kiosk and Internetmarketing. He says you'll spend at least $600 per week for rent.

Helpful Advices

Whether you lease or buy a cart depends on your product and location. In malls, you generally lease a cart from mall management. The cost of leasing depends on the season and mall traffic volume but is usually at least $800 per month for space and a cart, and can get very high in a good location. Some malls charge a percentage of your sales in addition to monthly rent.

Carts come in many sizes and styles with varying capabilities. There are carts for specific types of food, some with refrigerators, grills, steamers-- even small ovens so you can bake on location.

Think versatility, especially with food. Don't limit yourself to making one item, in case it doesn't sell well and you have to switch gears. You can get a good deal on used carts, but Clark, who also sells custom-designed carts, urges caution. "People buy a cart they think is cute--only to find out they've purchased someone else's headache," she says. "It ends up costing more to modify than to buy new."

Choosing a location really comes down to one key element: "It starts with identifying who your target customer is. You want to locate close to where those customers are," says Howard Van Auken, academic director for the Pappajohn Center for Entrepreneurship at Iowa State University in Ames.

With shopping center leases, you're customarily charged for maintenance of common areas and for the mall's marketing efforts. Find out what the mall's plans are for any structural alterations or remodeling, resurfacing the parking lots, or replacing the roof. These can be devastating assessments for a young business. Requirements for hours and days of operation, employee parking restrictions, participation in community service events, gift certificate and loyalty programs, and storefront appearance may not fit into your business plan or capabilities. Make sure you'll be capable of conforming to these requirements.

Cost

Costs can change according to your wishes. As I said above, its rent can be change between 600 or 800 dollars per month but if you want to be in a mall you need to rent 9.000 dollars, too. You can learn it from the local authorities.

Epilogue

Today, with the development of technology, life has begun to change completely. Of

course, our revenue and earnings sources are also influenced by it. If you want to

keep pace with these technological developments and earn more at the same time,

you can try your way to profit from the internet. Or you can change your business

area using government support and bank loans. All of this is in your hands.

But before you think about evaluating the business opportunities that I have

compiled for you in this article, you should make a very detailed plan. Do all the

research. Identify everything you need and make sure you are in compliance. Because

this new job opportunity will change your life, maybe you will do it all your life. If you

make a clear decision, be determined and believe in yourself.